Contents

Race – myth or reality?

Opposite A multiracial crowd – black, white and brown races? Or merely one race – the human race, with a variety of different-coloured skins?

Most people take it for granted that all humankind can be divided into races, and that scientists have established what 'race' is. For the vast majority, the evidence of their own eyes is enough. They *see* the different races in the variety of skin colour, hair type and facial shape shown by the people of the world.

The classification of races often found in books on the history and variety of the human species essentially follows this line of thinking. The main categories usually listed are the negroid/African, the mongoloid/Oriental and the caucasoid/European.

Scientifically invalid? Classifications of this nature have a long history (see pp 54-55). Yet many scientists today, if asked what 'race' is, would answer unequivocally that there is no such thing. They say that the concept of 'human races' is scientifically discredited and invalid.

The description of races always begins with physical characteristics. Yet there is no human physical attribute which has been proved always to be related to any other. Black skin, for example, is not always associated with a broad nose, nor with any other facial or body characteristic such as height or build. Even more important, there is no physical characteristic which is consistently related in any way to mental or behavioural attributes.

It is not possible to draw a line establishing scientifically where one race ends and another begins. Many people have argued, therefore, that the word 'race' should no longer be used in any context. Firstly, because it is meaningless; secondly, because the belief in 'races' historically has gone hand in hand with the most vicious practices against sections of the human population, and so can be considered an actively dangerous word. But opinions differ on this.

A social reality? Although some would say that the concept of 'race' has no scientific validity, people still believe it exists – thinking of themselves and others in these terms, and acting accordingly. A kind of reality thus emerges, a social reality, which can be called race. The relationships between peoples of different 'race' groups have come to be called 'race relations'.

Others argue, just as forcefully, that using these terms reinforces wrong ideas and encourages racist practice and thinking. It gives support to something which is in fact no more than a myth. According to the sociologist, Michael Banton, the vocabulary of 'race relations ... carries the implication that individuals all belong in particular races that can be recognized by characteristics of a permanent or nearly permanent kind. In reality the groups that are identified by race are continually changing. The special insidiousness of racial categorization is that it appears natural, masking its social character.'

There may be another danger, too. By analysing conflict in terms of 'race relations', 'race conflict', 'racism', we may be ignoring more fundamental causes of conflict. Just because people call something a 'race relations' issue – is it necessarily so?

> '*Race is the witchcraft of our time, the means by which we exorcise demons.*'
> Dr Ashley Montagu, anthropologist

'Races? That's just different colours – black, white, Asians . . .'

Black teenage girl

Are there

We can all see physical differences between human groups – colour, facial shape, hair, body build. Beyond these external features, however, no one has ever proved consistent differences of any kind.

Does blood matter? People sometimes believe different races have different blood – reflected in phrases like 'mixed-blood'. Yet it is impossible to tell a person's blood group from their physical appearance, and there is no consistent relationship between physical characteristics and the nature of a person's blood. Scientists say that the blood of all human groups is the same. It varies only in the frequency with which certain chemical components occur in different populations.

There is no direct relationship, either, between a person's genes and their physical make-up. Different, physically similar, peoples do not necessarily have the same combination of genes. 'All humankind shares the same basic storehouse of genes,' says Peter Farb in *Humankind*. And, according to Professor Bentley Glass, in *Genes and the Man*, 'It is unlikely there are many more than six pairs of genes in which the white race differs … from the black. Whites or blacks, however, unquestionably often differ among themselves by a larger number than this … a fact which reveals our racial prejudices as biologically absurd.'

To classify or not? Some biologists and anthropologists nevertheless believe that people can be classified into groups which they call races. The systems they use range from having three major divisions – mongoloid/caucasoid/negroid – through to some containing over 200 races.

But one of the most common problems is shown by a system which has nine major races and over thirty which are described as 'puzzling' or 'marginal'. Critics argue that the migration and mixing of peoples throughout history renders meaningless any attempt to split humans into series of clearly defined types, whether or not these are called 'races'.

Intelligence Some scientists, using intelligence tests as a measure, have said that white and black people have different levels of intelligence.

But the vast majority of experts reject these claims: intelligence tests, they say, do not measure innate ability – merely an instance of educational performance at that particular time, which can be affected by a vast range of environmental influences.

> '*It is wholly probable that true Negroes have a slightly lower average intelligence than the whites or yellows.*' Professor Sir Julian Huxley, biologist

racial differences?

Most scientists also agree that there is no possible reason why there should be a difference in intelligence between different ethnic groups. All human groups have had to develop mental qualities in order to survive. All groups now living are successful survivors. How can there be any fundamental difference in their intelligence?

We are left then with proven differences which are literally skin deep. Whether these differences matter or not probably depends, most of all, on whether you want them to.

'There is no evidence that any people is either biologically or mentally superior or inferior to any other people.'
Dr Ashley Montagu, anthropologist

Classifiers of human types find it impossible to fit everyone into their selected categories. Compare the features of this African girl (far left), often classified as negroid, with those of the Portuguese women (left), usually described as caucasoid.

acism could be described as a set of attitudes about another ethnic group, usually viewing them as 'worse' than one's own. It may be shown only as a fear or dislike of difference.

At the other end of the scale, it is a full-blown theory about the inferiority and superiority of different races, usually accompanied by prescriptions for 'protecting' one's own – most of which have resulted in violence and deprivation for the group subjected to the racism.

Manifestations of racism Racism shows itself in people's attitudes and beliefs – that is, as prejudice; and in actions against the people who are the objects of the racism – that is, as discrimination. Discrimination can affect access to and standards of jobs, housing, schooling and other social conditions. Or, as in the case of the German Nazi policies against the Gypsies and the Jews, it can lead to violence, even mass murder.

What causes racism? Some say that, throughout history, people have tended to assume that their own culture is superior and that others are inferior. The Chinese and Japanese, for example, have traditionally viewed Western culture as vastly inferior to

'There never was a civilized nation of any other complexion than white.'
David Hume, philosopher, 1771

Local government at work in a multiracial society. Hidden pressures, from early education on, may mean that members of certain ethnic groups never obtain some kinds of jobs. Yet it is often impossible to assess how much this is the result of class and economic barriers, rather than discrimination because of ethnic origin.

the mind?

their own, and the Ancient Romans believed that the peoples of the rest of Europe, particularly of Britain, were barbaric and uncivilized.

Others argue a much more specific cause for racism: 'Racism is linked to ... economic advantage and political domination,' say Baum and Coleman, in their analysis of the Christian Church's experience of racism around the world. Many would agree, arguing for example that white racism against blacks arose out of Europeans' seizure and plunder of territories in America, Asia and Africa, colonialism and slavery, and the European need to justify this abuse of peoples and their lands.

Others, however, have documented racist attitudes long before this, and have suggested the influence of Christianity, with its drive to convert, and its belief in the immorality and backwardness of non-Christian 'heathen' religions.

What, however, about prejudices between different groups of the same colour – between different tribes in Africa or different castes in India, against the Jews in many European societies at different times in history, or against certain groups (in Britain, for example against the Irish)? These prejudices are often expressed in blatantly racist terms. And what makes some individuals in a society racist, while others, in the same society, are not?

Are people born racist? Is everyone born with a fear of difference? Some would argue yes, and cite examples to prove it. Yet there is a lot of evidence that prejudice is learned, that a young child first displays it when it starts to absorb attitudes from adults.

'I've got nothing against them, really, but I'd rather there weren't any living next door.'
Sri Lankan (living in London) about Africans

Psychology, personality traits, family history, religion – all of these have been put forward as reasons for an individual's racism. One problem is that conflicts are often swiftly described as 'racial' when there may be other underlying causes.

Some have argued that economic conflict through the centuries between oppressed and oppressing groups is the root cause of some so-called 'racial' conflicts. With time, the class relationship has altered, leaving only the legacy of mistrust between the groups. Is this conflict, then, the result of 'racism'? Or indeed, is everything described as 'race prejudice' actually *inspired* by racism?

The language

Racism is often revealed in the language people use: explicit, extreme or offensive. Racist vocabulary may draw parallels with animals (such as pigs or apes), or contrast good and evil, morality and degeneracy, dirtiness and cleanliness, purity and impurity.

Racism may appear in a choice of words which betrays attitudes about the use and abuse of the victim, like the white citizen of an African country who claimed he didn't need a washing machine because, 'I've got a black one' – a very different statement from 'I employ someone to do the washing by hand.'

> **'The screaming idiotic words and savage music of these negro records are undermining the morals of our white youth.'**
> *American poster against jazz, 1920*

Hidden forms Yet the language of prejudice may also be a more subtle influence. It can form the central core of ideas and information yet never openly show the prejudiced standpoint from which judgments are made. Visual images, advertising, children's books and pictures, toys, geography and history books, newspaper, television and radio reporting, may all put forward standards about what is 'normal' and 'abnormal', suggest that unfamiliar things are suspect, imply that the norms of your own culture are held by everyone in the world. In children's books, phrases like 'strange' food, 'weird' clothes, physical descriptions of foreigners which talk of 'abnormal' or 'unusual' shapes (not merely shapes which are different from your own), all may present a continuous stream of suggestions about what is acceptable or desirable.

In addition, the way information is presented may encourage beliefs about the unequal capacity for development and 'civilization' in different peoples: the geography book which only ever shows hand agricultural tools used in Africa and gigantic combine harvesters in America or Europe; which suggests, as communities to be compared, the large urban community in Europe and the small rural community in Africa or Asia; which consistently shows poverty and squalor in the latter, without ever including reference to the fact that poverty can be found in most societies – and that America and Europe are no exceptions.

None of these may be racist in intention, yet many experts feel that they will reinforce stereotyped images of 'backwardness' or primitiveness and suggest an inability to 'move with the times' in other countries. By extrapolation, this is applied to the people of those other countries, when they appear in your own country.

Apparently innocent language may hide other prejudices. Words like 'immigrant', when referring to a group whose ancestors immigrated but who are themselves born and bred in the country; or its counterpart, the idea of a 'host' community – implying that the newer group is somehow perpetually a guest and therefore, presumably, at some time going to leave. And what about the word 'minority'? How often is it used to imply, subtly, that a group has less than full rights in a place?

> **'I am haunted by the human chimpanzees I saw along that hundred miles of horrible country.'**
> *Charles Kingsley,*
> *writing about the Irish in Ireland, 19th century*

# of prejudice

A German anti-semitic cartoon from the 1930s. Note the implied malpractice shown by the mincing of the rat. What else does the cartoon suggest?

Myths and

Racial myths and stereotyping usually link the physical characteristics of people to their behaviour – their morals, standards of achievement and civilization, even to their standards of living. Here is a fairly typical racial myth from the early 1800s. In 1810, the *Encyclopaedia Britannica* said of the negro: 'Vices the most notorious seem to be the portion of this unhappy race ... They are an awful example of the corruption of man left to himself.'

One modern form of the 'corruption and savagery of black people' myth is the image of gun-toting terrorists, for example in southern Africa. In news reports, films and stories, they are treated quite differently from the underground fighters against Nazi invaders in Europe during the Second World War. Yet these African fighters would call themselves liberation fighters in as just a cause – freeing their countries from interference and control by a 'fascist' foreign power – and many independent observers agree with them.

The American Indian One of the most durable myths is the image of the savage Red Indian, killing and maiming indiscriminately for the pleasure of increasing his collection of scalps. Yet it was the British government, in proclamations like the one quoted on this page, which established the system of scalping.

In the 1600s and 1700s settlers from Europe flooded in to the Indian territory of the North American continent. Their pursuit of land and gold met fierce opposition from Indian nations defending their lives and their livelihood. Settler groups and the American army met any opposition from the Indians with unmitigated savagery and brutality.

In 1927 the Grand Council Fire of American Indians said: 'We do not know if school histories are pro-British, but we do know that they are unjust to the life of our people – the American Indian. They call all white victories, battles, and all Indian victories, massacres.

'For every scalp of a male Indian brought in as evidence of their being killed ... forty pounds.'

Proclamation by King George III, 1775

caricatures

'White men call Indians treacherous – but no mention is made of broken treaties on the part of the white man.

'White men call Indians thieves – and yet we lived in frail skin lodges and needed no locks or iron bars. White men call Indians savages. What is civilization? Its marks are a noble religion and philosophy, original arts, stirring music, rich story and legend. We had these.'

You will not find in many books or films the true story of what the settlers (immigrants) did to the Indians in America. Yet the details are as gruesome as any story of Nazi brutality. The alternative viewpoint, however – the myth – is recreated daily in films, books, comics, toys, games.

Why then, do these myths arise? How and why are they created? And by whom?

Below and *opposite* The image of the savage, scalp-hunting Red Indian is a racial myth daily recreated in books, films, comics and toys. In reality, the Amerindians learned the practice of scalp-hunting from white bounty hunters.

Is slavery

There has been slavery for thousands of years. It existed in the ancient world, and continued until the Atlantic slave trade in Africans started in the early sixteenth century. Slavery had existed for a long time in African societies, and African slaves had for centuries been taken by Arab traders to serve in Arabia, India and Iran, under very brutal conditions.

The origin of racism? Most writers, however, regard the Atlantic slave trade (see pp 58-59) as fundamentally different from all previous forms of slavery. Many argue further, that it was here that racism originated. Previously, those taken in slavery had been of all ethnic groupings and all colours. They were war captives, people in debt, those who had sold themselves into slavery because of poverty –

for slaves were guaranteed food and lodging by their owners. They were owned, but were still regarded as people, with certain rights, including the right to buy their freedom.

On the other hand, slaves for the Atlantic trade were all black – all from Africa – and all to serve white masters. Although African and Arab merchants were partners in the trade, it was the demands of white men that prompted it. Equally important, this traffic in humans was seen as a trade in things – objects totally without rights of any kind. Many experts believe that racism developed as a justification for this: people could tell themselves it was all right, because the victims were sub-human.

Others argue the reverse, however: that it was because of racist ideas about Africans

Slaves at work on a West Indies sugar plantation in 1844. Was this slavery prompted by the need for cheap plantation labour – or by racist attitudes to the African people?

'Your bodies, you know, are not your own; they are at the disposal of those you belong to.'
Bishop's sermon to slaves, 18th century

14

to blame?

that, when the need for plantation labour arose, the traders looked to societies already defined as inferior.

Economic motives? Many people maintain that there were strong economic reasons for the slave trade and the way it was conducted. Slaves were needed for an economic purpose – to work. The denial of rights, the harshness of treatment, were motivated simply by the drive for maximum profit at minimum cost. Africans were seized because there was a ready supply available – African and Arab merchants were prepared to trade, and the rivalries in African societies prevented united opposition.

Some historians also argue that the link between slavery and racism is by no means a straightforward matter of cause and effect.

While the two certainly came together in the end, it was more than 150 years before those justifying the slave trade began to use racist arguments – and such views were already circulating before they were taken up by the slave trade's supporters.

There is equally much evidence that in the ancient world whites had positive and respectful attitudes about blacks, and intermarriage was not infrequent. Black gods and goddesses are part of the mythology of the Ancient Greeks, for example, alongside and equal to their white deities.

Yet in the late eighteenth century, theories about the moral and intellectual inferiority of darker-skinned peoples began to gain a wide currency. 'Black' came to be synonymous with 'slave'. It left an unmistakable legacy.

A slave rebellion in Jamaica in 1860. History books often suggest that slavery was abolished because of opposition from humanitarians. But slavery was also becoming a more inefficient way of producing goods, not least because it was increasingly costly and difficult to control the slaves.

The white man's

Many experts consider that the attitudes which developed among European colonizers about the peoples they subjugated are one of the historical roots of racism. How, then, did the colonizers see themselves and their role?

Bringing light? The quotation from Bismarck on the opposite page is taken from a speech he made at a conference in Berlin to establish an international private association to control the area around the Congo River in West Africa.

It encapsulates one of the central arguments about the benefits of European rule which were voiced throughout the 'scramble for Africa', as European nations fell over each other in their efforts to seize territories. This task of bringing 'light' (civilization, commerce, education, communications, technology) to the 'dark continent' of Africa was defined as the 'white man's burden' – the 'necessary and (selfless) burden of raising the black peoples to the status of humanity.'

Missionary societies, in their struggle to obtain finance for their work abroad, gave

A Mohawk Indian village in America, *circa* 1780. We are often told of the 'primitive' peoples found by Europeans in other parts of the world. Yet how would this village compare with a contemporary rural settlement in Europe?

burden?

much publicity to the 'abject' state of the natives, the 'moral squalor' in which they languished, their 'savagery and depravity' – all of these being synonymous with 'heathen' religions from which, the missionaries claimed, the natives must be rescued.

A bread and butter question? Other colonists argued a rather different reason for the seizure of territories. Cecil Rhodes, one of the architects of British rule in Southern Africa, said in 1895: 'I was in the East End of London yesterday and attended a meeting of the unemployed. I listened to the wild speeches and on my way home became more than convinced of the importance of imperialism ... In order to save the 40,000,000 inhabitants of the United Kingdom from a bloody civil war, we colonial statesmen must acquire new lands to settle the surplus populations, to provide new markets for the goods produced in the factories and mines.'

Speaking in 1923, Lord Lugard, another architect of British colonial rule in Africa, explained: 'The partition of Africa was, as we all recognized, due primarily to the economic necessity of increasing the supplies of raw materials and food to meet the needs of the industrialized nations of Europe.'

Was it racism? Colonization, then, was seen either as bringing light, or as solving domestic problems. In both lines of argument, there is an obvious disregard for the views, the culture and the needs of the people who already inhabited the seized territories. Some define this as racism. An interesting question to ponder is whether attitudes would have been any different had those countries been inhabited by whites. And how does it compare with the Nazis' seizure of land for settlement in central and eastern Europe before and during the Second World War?

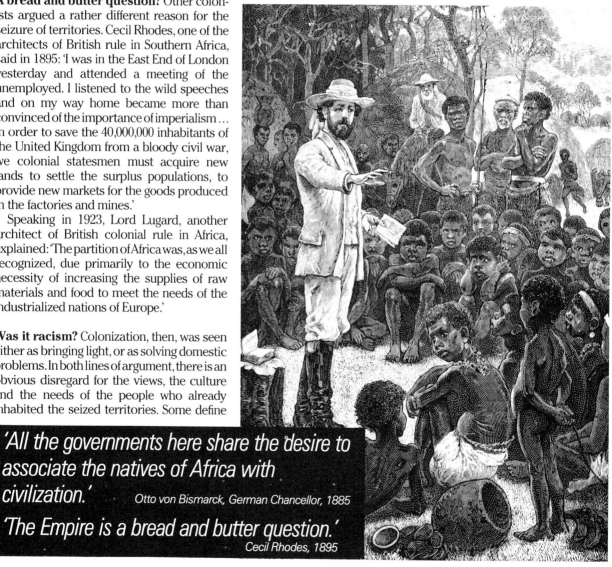

Missionaries widely publicised their 'civilizing' work among African peoples. This ran parallel to the invasion of the continent for economic motives.

'All the governments here share the desire to associate the natives of Africa with civilization.'
Otto von Bismarck, German Chancellor, 1885

'The Empire is a bread and butter question.'
Cecil Rhodes, 1895

The benefits

The two quotations below epitomize the conflicting opinions about the impact of colonial rule on the colonized peoples. Yet the African teacher, praising the Kaiser's rule, was writing only three years after a war in which the people of southern Tanzania had risen against the Germans, who controlled the land at the time. The rebellion was brutally crushed, using African troops from tribes which were no part of the uprising. (It has been estimated that 100,000 people died in the fighting and the ensuing famine.)

> 'Formerly our condition was one of injustice; but now there is peace everywhere.'
>
> *African teacher in southern Tanzania, 1909*

> 'All that the native has seen in his country is that they can freely arrest him, beat him, starve him.'
>
> *Frantz Fanon, 1961*

Real benefits? In all colonial societies, there were groups of colonized people (often educated in colonial mission schools) who embraced the religion and the civilization of the colonizing country willingly and who lauded what were seen as its benefits. The benefits most often cited included education and literacy (schools were opened to train clerks for the colonial service), public health programmes and the control of endemic diseases, and communications such as railways, roads and bridges.

Or destruction and dislocation? Others, however, describe a different process. They talk of the economies of colonized countries being geared only to the needs of their colonizers. This left a legacy of imbalance which

# of civilization?

remains long after independence from the colonial power (see p. 57).

(see p. 57)

In his preface to *The Wretched of the Earth* by Frantz Fanon, the French philosopher Jean Paul Sartre wrote: 'Violence in the colonies does not only have for its aim the keeping of these enslaved men at arm's length; it seeks to dehumanize them. Everything will be done to wipe out their traditions, to substitute our language for theirs and to destroy their culture without giving them ours.'

In *The Wretched of the Earth*, Frantz Fanon documents how a combination of physical exhaustion, starvation, illness and fear can destroy the spirit of a colonized people. The farmer is forced at gunpoint to accept the seizure of his land, and to work that land in the service of the colonizers: 'If he shows a fight, the soldiers fire and he's a dead man; if he gives in, he degrades himself and is a man no more.'

Many other writers show how the effects of this process are painfully exorcised in the overthrow of colonial rule and afterwards.

No consent? In 1961 President Julius Nyerere of Tanzania wrote: 'Our whole existence has been controlled by people with an alien attitude to life …A man who tries to control the life of another does not destroy the other any the less because he does it, as he thinks, for the other's benefit.'

For many colonized peoples, the situation is perhaps best summed up in the African saying: 'When they first came, they had the Bible and we had the land. We now have the Bible and they have our land.'

In New Zealand, two faces of civilization – settler-style.
Far left Maori women cover their nakedness with Victorian dresses.
Left Maoris, captured for resisting the seizure of their land by settlers, are herded on to a prison ship.

'The myth of white superiority is rebuilt in schools.'

Chris Proctor in Racist Textbooks

Teaching racism?

One of the central arguments about how racist views are created and perpetuated is that they are fed to us willy nilly in the information we receive about ourselves and others, particularly about history.

Many examples are given: phrases such as 'Columbus discovered America'; or the continent of Africa pictured only as emerging from being the 'dark continent' with the arrival of European missionaries and colonizers. Neither of these portraits is accurate. The Americas had been discovered thousands of years before, by the ancestors of the people already living there when Columbus and his sailors arrived. The Spaniards themselves came into contact, among others, with the peaceful communities of Arawaks, and the wealthy and highly-organized civilizations of the Aztecs in Mexico and the Incas in Peru. All three were wholly destroyed by the Spaniards. Yet this perspective is often missing when the history of these times is recounted, particularly for young children.

Enter the myths In his survey *Racist Textbooks*, Chris Proctor cites another example, that of Manhattan Island being bought from the American Indians for only a few dollars. A comparison of this with its present value is often used as evidence of the stupidity of the Indians: 'Yet to the Indian, the notion of a person *owning* land was ridiculous. The land cannot belong to one person, and why should one want to own it? The sale of Manhattan Island was a joke in Indian eyes. Somebody gave them four dollars to buy what cannot be possessed. It was like buying the sun to a European. Enter the "thick Indian" myth.'

As far as Africa is concerned, the balance is only slowly and intermittently adjusted with alternative information – about the diversity of cultures and highly-organized civilizations which existed in Africa long before white people ever set foot on the continent. Some believe, as a result of archaeological evidence, that Africa is in fact the cradle of humanity – that it was here that upright walking, intelligent humans first developed, and learned the skills necessary to start controlling their environment.

Deliberately racist? Many argue that history teaching is often actively racist both in intention and effect. They claim that it is stimulated by the belief that the original peoples of non-white countries were unable to advance before the arrival of white people.

Others take the view that it is more worrying if such attitudes among teachers and others are not *intentionally* racist, and are held by people who believe they are not racist in any way. The distortion of perspective must then be so ingrained that it simply flows out as an integral part of all their thought and judgment, without them realizing it. This, it is argued, is a significant part of the process by which racist thinking is bred in young people, both white *and* black.

Opposite The ruins of Great Zimbabwe, capital of a wealthy African kingdom which stretched across present-day Mozambique, Zambia and Zimbabwe. It was at its height long before the first Europeans reached Africa in the sixteenth century. When European explorers first saw the ruins, they believed they must have been built by a non-African civilization.

This is the face of Africa most often shown in textbooks, while other aspects of current life there are ignored.

Anti-semitism had been a thread in German society long before the Nazis came to power in 1933. However, they elevated it to a central policy during the 1930s and early 1940s, ultimately practising genocide in the mass extermination of Jewish people in concentration camps, in what they called 'the final solution of the Jewish question'.

Nazi theories Intellectual traditions, like those of the nineteenth-century French writer, Count Joseph de Gobineau, were the foundation of Nazi racism. Gobineau's central opinion was that 'history shows that all civilization flows from the white race'. The 'jewel' of the white race was said to be the Aryans (although who these were was never clearly defined). In

A Nazi election poster depicting the Jew as the 'string-puller', manipulating the German people.

'The Jew is the corrupter of our nation.'
Adolf Hitler

the Nazi development of this theory, the Germans were the true inheritors of Aryan blood.

The divisions within German society were officially drawn up along these theoretical lines – between Aryan and non-Aryan. The chief categories of non-Aryan were defined as the Jews and the Gypsies.

But why? Hitler explained: 'My Jews are a valuable hostage given to me by the democracies. Anti-semitic propaganda in all countries is an almost indispensable medium for the extension of our political campaign. You will see how little time we shall need in order to upset the ideas of the whole world, simply and purely by attacking Judaism.'

Thus, creating scapegoats, shifting the blame for all problems onto a specific group, was raised to a central principle of Nazi policy. All left-wing and liberal opposition to the Nazis and all economic misery were attributed to a Jewish conspiracy. A forgery, *The Protocols of the Elders of Zion*, was produced, which claimed that an international Jewish conspiracy was aiming to take control of the white races first in Russia, then in Germany.

Nazism in action In August 1932, before the Nazis seized power, Hitler showed his real long-term objective by using his influence to gain the acquittal of five stormtroopers who had sadistically murdered a communist for his political views.

On coming to power in early 1933, the Nazis made their first moves. These were not against the Jews but against the trade unions and all political opposition. Trade union rights of association and collective bargaining were removed, trade union offices and assets seized, leaders arrested. By the spring of 1933, any form of organized opposition was crushed. This was achieved and maintained by creating a climate of hostility against other targets (the Jews) which deflected attention and opposition to the Nazis.

Then the official attack on the Jews began. There were boycotts of Jewish shops, lawyers

the Nazis?

and doctors; demands for the removal of Jewish pupils from schools and universities. In the latter half of the 1930s, 'Aryan origin' became a precondition for almost any employment. From 1938 onwards, the policy moved into full-scale pogroms, deportations, imprisonments and, finally, extermination.

A means to an end? Nearly all Fascist movements in the 1930s in Germany, Italy, Britain, France and Spain were violently anti-semitic. Why? Was anti-semitism itself the objective? Or was it a means to an end – the means by which, to paraphrase Hitler, 'the people's attention is consolidated against a single adversary so that nothing will split up their attention' – the means by which the Nazis established their control?

The Nazis' final solution: the bodies of Jewish victims found when Bergen Belsen concentration camp was opened up.

'The art of leadership consists in consolidating the attention of the people against a single adversary.' *Adolf Hitler in* Mein Kampf

A new

any people are worried that the type of racism found in the Fascist parties before and during the Second World War is continuing and spreading.

Others, however, consider there is a more real and dangerous problem: a new form of racist theory, many of whose exponents would firmly deny the title 'racist', and who argue that they do not have a belief in the innate superiority of one race over another. What they do have is merely 'a concern about conflict born of the cultural difference between people'.

Their views may be paraphrased like this: 'Rightly or wrongly, people have *genuine* worries which must be taken account of. People *believe* their way of life and culture is threatened, therefore policies must be formulated which will allay their fears.'

Being swamped? In 1978, future Prime Minis-

A National Front march in Britain claims that the black community are the source of many problems, while young girls link arms in a counter-demonstration.

'The cultural roots of this new racism have encouraged making the black community an easy scapegoat for wider political failure.'

Peter Hain, Young Liberals

racism?

ter Margaret Thatcher said, 'People are really rather afraid that this country might be swamped by people with a different culture'; the view of politician William Whitelaw was that 'Many genuine people, entirely free from racial prejudice, want reassurance'.

Views like these are seen by some people as forming a kind of racism which is more subtle than the Nazi brand, and all the more dangerous because it is 'respectable'. In *The New Racism*, Martin Barker explains how such racism can exist without using insults: 'It need never talk of "niggers", "wogs" or "coons". It does not need to see Jews as morally degenerate, or blacks as "jungle bunnies". Nonetheless, in subtle but effective ways, it authorizes the very emotions of hostility that then get expressed in these terms.'

He goes on to outline how 'the new racism is a theory of human nature', which says that people are naturally aware of their differences from other groups or nations. They do not necessarily think of them as better or worse. They simply do not want outsiders to be admitted.

The view is epitomized by comments such as the following, from another British politician, Winston Churchill, during a parliamentary debate on immigration in 1976: 'We cannot fail to recognize the deep bitterness that exists among ordinary people who one day were living in Lancashire, and woke up the next day in New Delhi, Calcutta or Kingston, Jamaica.'

Shifting the blame? It is argued that through such views as these, articulated by politicians and the media, a climate of opinion is created within which attacking specific communities becomes respectable. These communities are identified as the source of ills, so that eradicating the community (for example by repatriation to their country of origin) is presented as a way of removing the ills.

These opinions may avoid the Nazi style – but do they differ in essence from the way the Nazis made scapegoats of the Jews? And where did that lead?

> 'The whole question of race is not a matter of being superior or inferior, dirty or clean, but of being different.'
>
> Robin Page, Daily Telegraph, 1977

Is this

The examples of prejudice and discrimination most often cited are those by whites against blacks. But they are not the only ones.

Tensions and conflict described by outsiders and participants as 'racial' exist in many other situations – between Africans and Asians in East and Central Africa; between West Indians and Asians in some parts of the Caribbean; between different groups of Africans (of different tribal origin) in Africa; between Europeans of Gentile and Jewish origin; between Jews of European and Arab origin in Israel; between people of different religions throughout the Indian sub-continent. In many European countries, Gypsies, or Roma, are the victims of often violent discrimination.

The conflicts take many forms, often cultural (particularly religious) and economic, and produce antagonisms that are centuries-old. One problem in assessing them is that it is never very clear in what sense these conflicts are described as 'racial' as opposed to, for example, 'class' or 'religious' conflicts.

Sri Lanka There are, for example, recurring bouts of communal violence between the Tamil and the Sinhalese people in Sri Lanka (formerly known as Ceylon). Burning, looting and killing take place, and many hundreds have died each time, the vast majority of them Tamils. Tamils are the minority people on the island, and are predominantly Hindu. The majority Sinhalese people are Buddhists.

For centuries the Sinhalese have considered the Tamils as 'heathen invaders': 'This bright, beautiful island was made into a paradise by the Aryan Sinhalese before its destruction was brought about by the barbaric vandals,' wrote the historian Anagarika Dharmpala in 1902.

In 1983 there was widespread communal violence throughout Sri Lanka.
Right Shops in the centre of the capital, Colombo, were ransacked.
Opposite Thousands of Tamil refugees are guarded by soldiers.

racism?

Prejudiced from an early age? Tamil and Sinhalese children show early prejudices. 'Every child is taught in his or her mother tongue. This results in the segregation in schools of the two races, the Sinhalese and the Tamils. Differences of race are ingrained in the Sinhalese child's mind, and even playtime sees them grouping themselves according to race,' reported the Ceylon Institute of National and Tamil Affairs (CINTA) to the International Commission of Jurists in 1974.

As the Tamils see it, in the words of Mr Amirthalingham, leader of the Tamil United Liberation Front, in 1978: 'The two nations continue to live apart ... the majority nation has been enthroned in the seat of power and the minority nation has been made a subject nation.'

The main focus of recent conflict has been whether the Tamil language will be used as a second national language alongside Sinhala. Some Sinhalese fear they will be swamped: 'The fact that in the towns and villages most of the work is in the hands of the Tamil-speaking people will inevitably result in fear of the inexorable shrinking of the Sinhalese language,' said politician Mr Bandaranaika, in a speech to the House of Representatives.

Can such situations be compared with other examples of 'racial' conflict described in this book? What other cases can you think of?

> 'The policy of the government is the eventual liquidation of the Tamils as a racial minority and their absorption into the Sinhalese community.'
>
> CINTA, 1974

Mixing

The possible degrees of racial mixing range from segregation (complete separateness in one or all spheres), through integration (in theory a mixing and cooperation between equal partners), to assimilation (the absorption of a group, its culture and way of life, and even, through sexual mixing over many generations, of its colour).

Problems arising out of cultural differences such as religion can exist, of course, quite independently of race prejudice. It is probably as difficult for an atheist to live at close quarters with a strict Roman Catholic family as for a Christian to live as part of a Moslem family; or for liaisons to take place across Hindu/Moslem, Moslem/Buddhist or Christian/Jewish boundaries, when both sides are firm believers. There may be fundamental disagreements about how family life should be conducted, the upbringing of children, and social and family priorities.

> '*Ethnic group mixture constitutes one of the greatest creative powers in the progress of mankind.*'
>
> Dr Ashley Montagu, anthropologist

The myth of blood The most controversial aspect of racial mixing is often sexual mixing – inside or outside marriage. It is here that the question of blood, what has been called by some writers the 'blood myth', assumes importance. This is the belief that the blood of offspring will be contaminated by the blood of the other group.

Nazis held this opinion; and it is one of the ostensible justifications for South Africa's laws against 'mixed' sexual relations and marriages. Scientifically, however, it is a myth (see pp 6-7). There is no biological reason why mixing of different groups should not take place, for humans are all of the same species. In a review of the evidence from studies of 'sexual crossings' between different ethnic groups, Dr Ashley Montagu concludes that, 'Far from being deleterious to the generations following them, interbreeding between different ethnic groups is highly advantageous to mankind.'

Social barriers? The barriers, then, would seem to be not biological but social. They are determined by prejudice, the belief in the harmfulness of such mixing, rather than its reality. The term 'half-caste' indicates the way in which people in this situation are frequently ostracised by both sides because of such prejudice.

races?

Yet throughout history different groups, on first encountering each other, have mixed freely. In many early colonial settlements, including South America and South Africa, sexual relations took place on a wide scale between the colonizers and the indigenous peoples. In South Africa the population now defined as 'coloured' was originally the offspring of the early Dutch settlers and the Africans of the area.

To take two examples at opposite ends of the scale. In Brazil, there has never been any social stigma attached to sexual mixing between, for example, the black population and the white. Over 400 years it has produced a much-mixed population, with considerable gradations of colour.

On the other hand, in South Africa, such mixing of the races is today forbidden by law. Yet illegal relationships and marriages continue at an increasing rate as people respond to each other as fellow humans, against the full weight of social prejudice and legal prohibition.

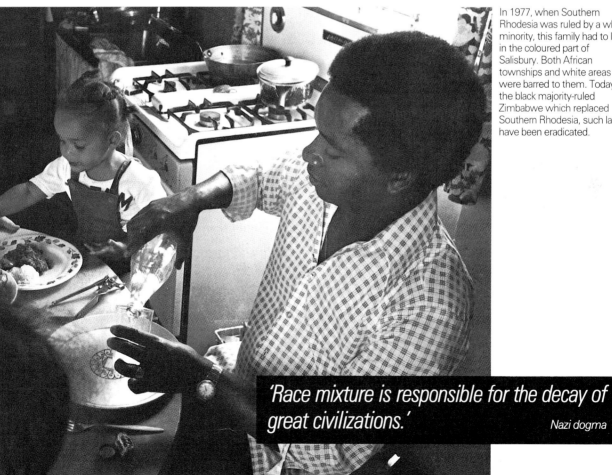

In 1977, when Southern Rhodesia was ruled by a white minority, this family had to live in the coloured part of Salisbury. Both African townships and white areas were barred to them. Today, in the black majority-ruled Zimbabwe which replaced Southern Rhodesia, such laws have been eradicated.

'Race mixture is responsible for the decay of great civilizations.'

Nazi dogma

Civil rights =

'I've seen the promised land.'
Rev. Martin Luther King, 1968

equality?

merica is often said to be a country where equality of opportunity for all citizens is now paramount – regardless of race, colour or creed – and where civil rights for black people were won in the early 1960s. These years saw the culmination of a long, bitter and bloody struggle against the injustices for black people which were the legacy of attitudes from the era of slavery. In the end a variety of new laws were won – the legal right to vote, and the outlawing of discrimination and segregation in schooling, housing and jobs.

Did anything change? Does this mean that black people in the United States now have equality in status, opportunity and conditions? The differences in American public life are seen by some as evidence of a substantial and continuing change. The number of black elected officials in the South rose from fewer than 100 in 1965 to around 5,000 in 1980. There are over 200 black Mayors in major cities. There are black Congress representatives, ambassadors, senior government officials, a black candidate for the presidency, black lawyers, teachers, bankers.

Others argue that this is a purely superficial change which masks the fact that racial discrimination is still deeply entrenched in the US – in government organizations, the civil service, churches, trade unions, professional organizations and education.

Segregation of schools, for example, was outlawed. Yet in the majority of areas, white children go to one school and blacks to another. Integrated schools are generally of poor quality. Poverty and bad housing are usual in black areas; one third of all black people still live on or below the official poverty line. Unemployment among blacks remains nearly twice as high as among whites.

Thus many writers argue that the battle for civil rights and the passing of new laws may have changed the hopes and expectations of the black population, but did not alter the basic economic and social conditions. Writing in 1981, Professor Harvard Sitkoff said: 'Black America in 1980 was radically different from what it had been in 1954. Yet the full promise of the civil rights revolution was unrealized. Prejudice, discrimination and segregation, both subtle and blatant, continued to poison social relations. Neither the franchise nor the demolition of legal racism resulted in equality or justice.'

Now the Ku Klux Klan, the organization responsible for many thousands of lynchings, is widely active again. Currently some 600 cases of violence are being reported each year.

How then is a 'right', supposedly guaranteed in law, to be translated into practice? How can it become more than just a principle and take on a full social and economic reality?

Opposite A massive civil rights march in America in the late 1960s demands an end to segregation in schools, housing and jobs. Dr Martin Luther King, wearing a badge, is in the centre foreground.

With America swept by civil rights protest, US athletes at the 1968 Olympic Games in Mexico give a Black Power salute.

'The black struggle did not result in racial equality.'
Professor Harvard Sitkoff

Separate –

Some people argue that segregation does not necessarily produce inequality. An example of segregation is South Africa – whose entire political, economic and cultural system is founded on the idea of 'separate development', known as apartheid. Supporters argue that under apartheid each race is able to achieve its full potential, and preserve its culture without risk of diluting it with outside influences. The aim, they say, is to ensure a separate, but equal, development of the different races in all spheres.

Another view is epitomized in these comments from Dr Malan, Leader of the Nationalist Party during the 1948 election campaign in South Africa. 'Apartheid,' he said, 'is a way of saving the white civilization from vanishing beneath the black sea of South Africa's non-European populations.' It was after this election, when Dr Malan became Prime Minister, that apartheid began.

Apartheid in action These are some of apartheid's laws: mixed marriages and sexual relations between white and non-white illegal; everyone racially classified as White, Bantu (African), Coloured or Asiatic; separate living areas for different races; separate transport, public amenities and facilities, health and medical care, schools and universities; all Africans to carry a pass; all Africans excluded from representation in the national Parliament; African political organizations and multiracial political organizations banned; house arrest or indefinite imprisonment without trial allowed on suspicion of opposing apartheid.

Economic parity? The whites are 20 per cent of South Africa's population. They have 87 per cent of the land. The Africans are 70 per cent of the population – 22 million people. They have 13 per cent of the land – the 'homelands', which are sited in the least developed areas of the country, least suitable for farming and some of them semi-desert. All rights to mine minerals (on which South Africa's wealth is founded) are reserved for the South African government.

Africans can leave their 'homelands' to seek temporary work in the towns, but this is controlled by pass laws. 'The entire basis of our policy,' explains G. F. Van L. Froneman, Minister for Justice, Mines and Planning, 'is a system of migratory labour'.

During a demonstration against pass laws at Sharpeville in 1960, South African police opened fire on demonstrators, killing more than 50.

'Our people have been robbed of their birthright to land, liberty and peace.'
African National Congress, 1955

and equal?

The Africans who serve the industrial and commercial demands of Johannesburg live in Soweto, the largest of the black townships. South Africa is a wealthy country. Yet only 25 per cent of Soweto's houses have inside running water, 15 per cent of them have electricity, 7 per cent have a bath and 3 per cent hot water.

Medical and health-care facilities for the three non-white races are of a different standard from those for the whites. As a result African infants have a mortality rate six times higher than that of white infants.

In 1978, the Minister of Plural Relations and Development, Dr Connie Mulder said: 'There must be no illusions. If our policy is taken to its full, logical conclusion, there will not be one black man with South African citizenship.'

Is this a description of separate but equal development?

An official resettlement village in KwaZulu homeland, Natal, 1982. Millions of black South Africans have been forcibly moved to such villages since the introduction of apartheid in 1948.

'Each group will be able to develop into a self-sufficient unit.'
Dr Verwoerd, South African Minister of Native Affairs, 1948

'Degradation and discrimination ... are a simple fact of life for all Aborigines.'
Janine Roberts in From Massacres to Mining

Dispossessed?

The Aborigines of Australia are often cited as an example of a people whose existence, since the arrival of the first European settlers in Australia, has been conditioned entirely by racial prejudice. Others argue that, once again, this apparent racism is inextricably interwoven with the economic motives of the early settlers.

The main objective of the settlers was to acquire land. This meant seizing it from the people who were already there – the Aborigines, who in turn banded together to fight off the invaders. The resulting warfare, in which the Aborigines were massacred, lasted about 160 years. It came to an end when the colonial authorities decided to allocate temporary reserves for the Aborigines, but under the control of the authorities.

Secure reserves? Originally reserves were on land which was not wanted by the white settlers. More recently, however, there have been new attacks on Aboriginal land rights. In her book *From Massacres to Mining*, Janine Roberts talks of 'the dispossession of the Aborigines first by the military demands of the British and Australian authorities [to test nuclear bombs], then by the cattle companies, and finally by the transnational mining companies.' Important mineral deposits (uranium, for example) have been found on Aboriginal lands.

Conditions for Aborigines generally are explicitly discriminatory. Those living on reserves in Queensland may be expelled at any time by the manager. They can receive no visitors without permission, and are forced to do whatever work the manager requires. About half have their property controlled by the government, and cannot even draw money from their bank account without the government's permission.

Poverty and discrimination Without land, the Aborigines are forced to seek work. But government enquiries have established that few jobs, and then only the most menial, are ever offered to them, and that they are employed at the lowest wages in the country. They therefore suffer acute poverty and chronic malnourishment. In Sydney, for example, well endowed with health-care facilities, 25 per cent of Aboriginal children are seriously malnourished. Conditions in the rural areas are even worse.

Other official reports have highlighted the degree of prejudice and discrimination affecting nearly every aspect of Aboriginal life. They concluded: 'Aborigines remain the worst discriminated-against group in the Australian community.' Evidence has also been gathered of police shootings, brutality, cell beatings, false arrests and similar.

The Aborigines are now an entirely dispossessed people. Are they simply the victims of racism, as some believe?

Opposite The arrest of an Aborigine demonstrating in defence of land rights. Strong and continuing resistance from Aborigines has not stopped transnational companies from mining on their land, using open-cast methods which can poison the soil.

'Give them land and they'll soon want other privileges ... like wages, houses, self-respect, equality.' *From a cartoon by Honest in* The National Times, *1977*

Here

The debate about immigration is probably one of the oldest. It is a subject which poses basic questions for any country, regardless of the origin of the proposed immigrants.

What, for example, will be the impact of the new arrivals? Will there be an overall growth in size of population? If so, what will the impact be on social services, jobs, housing, education? What kind of immigration will it be – long or short term? What kind of commitment to the country are the immigrants intending to make? What kind of contribution will they be able to make? Are there special circumstances which should make your country allow them entry – as may be the case for refugees, or where there is a historical link between your country and theirs?

The racist connection? The whole question, however, can become inextricably linked with racist attitudes. It may be, for example, that one particular category of potential immigrants is allowed in, while others are kept out, purely on the grounds of their ethnic origin. It may be that some categories of immigrants are maltreated by immigration authorities, subjected to harassment, unnecessary scrutiny, indignities, even cruelties.

It may even be that communities who are settled, to the extent that second and third generations have been born and brought up in the new country, are still regarded as immigrants, with reduced rights.

In the opinion of many, the above applies entirely to the communities who migrated to Britain from the West Indies, India and Pakistan. Originally, an open-door policy allowed right of entry into Britain and citizenship to any person holding a British passport, including those issued in Commonwealth countries. This was subsequently altered, and such rights were conferred only on those who were born, adopted or naturalized in Britain, or whose parents were. From this time on all other potential immigrants were subjected to controls on entry and possible deportation.

Two classes of citizen? Many claim that two classes of British citizen have been created, the second class being those with black or brown skins.

The whole subject of immigration laws presents a tangled web of claim and counterclaim about racism. Some argue they have merely legitimate concerns about the rate of immigration and the impact on jobs and services. Others take issue with the statistics quoted, and believe there is no problem: the arguments, they say, are a smokescreen for opposition to immigration and existing immigrant communities of particular ethnic origin.

How then does a country go about determining and implementing sensible immigration policies which do not discriminate on the grounds of race, colour or creed, and which confer on those who are allowed to enter, and who decide to settle, full rights and freedoms as citizens?

> '*All those with foreign names or faces are subject to police and immigration surveillance.*'
> Stephen Castles in Here for Good

to stay?

Outside a mosque in Brick Lane, London. A community of settlers may face repeated demands to return to their country of origin, despite years of legitimate residence and contribution to their new country.

Guest

There are over 16 million migrant workers and their families now living in Western Europe. The migrants come mainly from the poorer European countries, or from former colonies. In countries other than Britain, migrants have a legal right only to temporary residence, and are known as 'guest workers'.

Racist hostility? There is much documented evidence that racism is a daily fact of life for members of these new ethnic minorities in Western Europe. Although they have the same colour skin as the indigenous majority, attitudes to them have all the hallmarks of prejudice and discrimination of a racial kind.

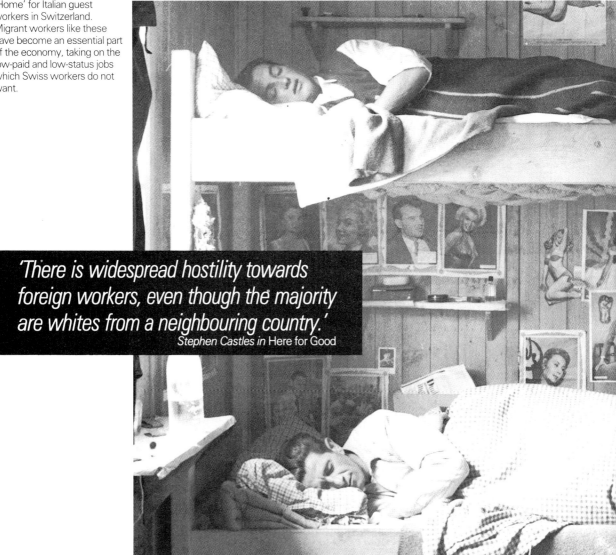

'Home' for Italian guest workers in Switzerland. Migrant workers like these have become an essential part of the economy, taking on the low-paid and low-status jobs which Swiss workers do not want.

'There is widespread hostility towards foreign workers, even though the majority are whites from a neighbouring country.'
Stephen Castles in Here for Good

workers?

Summarizing the situation in his book *Here for Good*, Stephen Castles wrote: 'Racism is on the upsurge in all the countries of immigration. Employers, politicians and the media promote the image of immigrants as the cause of the [economic] crisis, rather than as fellow victims. Immigrants no longer appear to be useful "guest workers" who do the dirty work, but as an alien and growing threat to culture and society.'

The Swiss system From 1945 onwards, Switzerland allowed foreign workers, mainly from Italy and, more recently, from Spain and Yugoslavia, to enter the country to work. By 1975, about a third of all workers and half of all factory workers were foreigners.

They came under a rigidly controlled 'guest worker' arrangement. The objective was to ensure that they came in response to Switzerland's labour needs and left again after a short time. Rapid turnover was the aim, with none of them settling in the country. Only a minimum number of their dependants was allowed in, and residence permits could be withdrawn at any time.

Two things happened: the migrants took up jobs with low pay and low status, so allowing most Swiss workers to move out of such employment. The immigrant workers thus became an essential part of the Swiss economy. At the same time, more and more stayed on. Settler communities became established, with second and third generations of children being born in Switzerland.

Refusing to acknowledge these developments, the Swiss government has done little to provide housing and social facilities. Restrictive controls on foreign residents continue. They can be deported for a variety of reasons, and to become a citizen requires 12 years' residency; combined with other requirements about language knowledge, this makes it prohibitive to most migrants.

General, widespread hostility towards foreign immigrants is reflected in recurrent public campaigns to expel foreign residents. This situation is paralleled in other European countries which have sizeable ethnic minorities.

Should countries run their economies with groups of foreign, migrant workers? If so, how can these groups be ensured fair treatment?

Second-class

Discrimination can take two main forms – informal; or formal and institutionalized, enshrined in the laws, practices and forms of authority by which a society is run.

A legal framework? Institutional discrimination may show itself, for example, in laws which discriminate against particular categories of people. Many writers have documented how, in Europe, migrant workers of all ethnic origins suffer institutional racism.

This not only manifests itself in the control of settlement rights, rights of entry into the country, employment and residence; once immigrants are legally in the country, they may still be denied political and civil rights – so that the group is kept in a position of inequality from which it is unable to participate fully in society. In effect, migrant workers are second-class citizens. This leads to a sense of insecurity; equally it may lead to deportation, detention without trial and family separation, on the grounds of infringement of one or other immigration laws.

Writing, for example, about the position of immigrants in Britain in *Race in Britain*, Gideon Ben-Tovim and John Gabriel said: 'There has been a gradual stripping away of the rights of black Commonwealth citizens whose enfranchised position has now been reduced to that of an alien contract labourer, subject to

> '*All human beings are born free and equal in dignity and rights.*' UN Universal Declaration of Human Rights

citizens?

a battery of administrative controls designed to make the entry of *black* ex-citizens and their families as arduous as possible.' Similar examples have been cited for a whole range of countries which have sizeable immigrant communities and which apply immigration controls.

The police? Institutional racism may also be expressed in the conduct of the police. Racist attitudes among the police may affect their work: a belief that immigrant communities commit a higher proportion of crimes (a belief not borne out by statistics) will inevitably affect the way in which police approach investigations in these communities. It may also affect their attitude to collecting evidence and interviewing witnesses.

Is this discrimination unique? Many would view this institutional racism as a special if not unique problem in society.

Others consider it as just yet another form of discrimination, which is ranged alongside discrimination against workers and trade union rights generally, against protest forms of politics, against women, against old people, against young people, against poor people. Police in many countries, for example, show a propensity for assuming that a young person is, by definition, disreputable and 'loitering with intent'.

Are these fundamentally different from institutional discrimination on the grounds of race? And does institutional racism require different solutions from the other forms of discrimination?

Opposite A National Front gathering in London, flanked protectively by the police, displays racist and anti-immigration banners.
Below In Manchester police hold back those who want to protest against a National Front march.

Creating

Examples abound of racist language and distorted selection of facts in newspaper, radio and television coverage, and in books. There are stories like that in the *Daily Mail* in 1978, headed 'Mobs unleash a wave of vengeance: white terror in Smith raid backlash'; or 'mobs of black Zambians, hysterical with fury'. Note the choice of vocabulary – 'white terror', the blacks described as 'hysterical mobs', not 'protesters' or 'demonstrators', or other more neutral phrases.

In addition, the ethnic origin of people is often included, or even emphasized, when it is irrelevant to the story. This is likely to give a distorted impression of the facts: crime stories where the perpetrators are from minority communities are a good example. Including reference to ethnic origin may reinforce, or even create, stereotyped images of the connection of this group with crime or with particular types of crime, such as street crime and mugging. This then has the effect of encouraging beliefs that particular ethnic communities are making the streets unsafe for other residents.

'[The media] define the situation as one of intergroup conflict.' C. *Critcher* et al *in* Ethnicity and the Media

Distorted selection? Distortion of information may result merely from the choice of what news to cover: conflicts between particular ethnic groups; a high profile for anti-immigrant organizations (implying thereby that they are numerically greater and more influential than they are). In all these ways, the media may not merely exacerbate existing racism, but actually create it.

prejudice?

Is race reporting unique? A variety of writers acknowledge that coverage of race-related issues follows the conventional pattern of the media's choice of 'newsworthy' stories. Conflict-oriented themes are the main interest, because they 'catch the attention'. This is also shown in the treatment of trade union affairs and workers' struggles generally.

Is racism in the media, then, a particular problem requiring special solutions? Or is it one aspect of a general problem that manifests itself in many different forms in the media of most countries – where 'newsworthiness' tends to rate above accuracy and objectivity, and selection of information for impact, or blatant misinformation, is frequent?

Are those generating media coverage guilty of conscious racism? According to Professor James D. Halloran of the Centre for Mass Communications Research, the treatment by the media of racial and ethnic issues 'is best seen as stemming from normal journalistic practices rather than as something unique or special to race'.

Does it matter? Few doubt the significance of the media in affecting relationships between different groups. Peter Tucker of the Commission for Racial Equality argued: 'The results of research show a clear relationship between the attitudes adopted by the public to various race-related issues and the way these are presented by the national as well as the local press and radio.'

Left In 1981, street disturbances in Brixton, London, were persistently labelled 'race riots' by the media, suggesting a community violently torn by racial hatred *between* blacks and whites. In fact the clashes were between the police on one hand and Brixton residents, including whites, on the other. Here a group help themselves to goods from a looted shop.

> *'The media's ideas of "race relations" are reproduced in public opinion.'*
> Barry Troyna in Public Awareness and the Media

Can laws

Both in Britain and in the United States, a legal framework now exists to outlaw discrimination in a wide variety of areas. These include employment, housing, the supply of goods, and the provision of other facilities and services.

'You can't legislate against prejudice.' *Teenager*

In the United States segregation was once the official policy in many southern States, and was applied to buses, schools, health facilities and many other spheres. This is now against the law. In Britain, race relations law also makes it illegal to use racially abusive language in a public place, or to publish anything which is threatening, abusive or insulting to a racial group, or likely to stir up hatred against them.

help?

Do laws work? This depends to a large extent on whether they can be enforced. Are there procedures and organizations through which complaints may be brought, and wrongs corrected and compensated? Does the compensation allowed include legal penalties? What redress is there against someone who simply ignores a judgment against them? Are procedures for invoking the laws likely to be used? Do people know about them? Are they

straightforward and manageable, without requiring substantial financial outlay or enormous legal preparation? All these questions have to be borne in mind when judging whether laws could work.

In the opinion of the Commission for Racial Equality (CRE) in Britain: 'In the short term, laws can only control behaviour. Much of our behaviour in public and in private is affected by law. But in the long term, the law will reduce racial prejudice by discouraging the behaviour in which prejudice finds expression.'

However, in countries where laws do exist, such as the US and Britain, observers generally agree that there has been neither an eradication nor even a significant reduction in discrimination (see p. 31). In Britain there are still some tens of thousands of acts of discrimination every year, according to the CRE.

Tokenism? One of the criticisms levelled at the legal solution, and the organizations set up to enforce it, is that they are often designed to make it *look* as if something is being done, and therefore encourage people to slacken pressure for change, while in effect very little is actually being done. Critics say that it can act as a policy to contain protest within manageable bounds, rather than to look for real, permanent solutions.

So what can be done? Most experts would argue that a combination of laws and education is the answer. Neither can be excluded and the two have to work in tandem. This of course raises other questions: what kind of laws, with what kinds of penalties attached for infringement; and what kind of education?

Left Pupils at a Los Angeles high school in the 1970s. Although segregation in US schools is now illegal, in practice it continues. Black pupils attend state schools boycotted by whites, while the majority of white parents send their children to private schools.

45

Positive

Opposite Scanning the vacancy lists is a soul-destroying task for the unemployed, whether young or old, black or white.

One of the suggestions for correcting discrimination against ethnic minorities is to discriminate 'positively' in their favour. In order to redress the imbalance in opportunity and lack of representation by an ethnic group, whether in housing, employment or education, some people suggest that positive measures should be taken to favour the group: preferential treatment when applying for jobs, reserved places in educational establishments, special resources to deal with various aspects of deprivation.

On the way to equality? Supporters of this solution do not argue that it represents equality of opportunity; but they say that the temporary reverse imbalance will, in time, correct itself so that true equality emerges. Once members of ethnic groups previously unrepresented, for example, in certain types of employment have done those jobs, then the tendency for them either not to apply or not to be offered the jobs (or both) will lessen.

Faced with decades of discrimination, just breaking through the barrier may be a significant contribution – not so much for the individual as for society in general. On the one hand, the community discriminated against sees that equality of opportunity is possible. Equally, the discriminating community will see positive results which will lessen prejudice and stereotyped beliefs.

Some critics are concerned about the loss of opportunity for those who are not in the relevant ethnic minority. This is defended as a necessary temporary loss. Others believe it is an error to accept that resources, jobs, housing are limited, and that one or other group must therefore go without. All resources to the deprived should be increased. It is not so much a question of a larger slice of the cake as a larger cake to share out, they say.

Unfair? To many, however, positive discrimination is merely inverted racial discrimination of essentially the the same kind as the one it intends to correct. However temporary, it is still undesirable. What, for example, about the candidate for a job, or house, who was equally qualified to receive it, but who in effect lost it merely on the grounds of race?

Others dislike positive discrimination because it is tokenism – it balances the books and makes the numbers look right, without actually dealing with the root causes of the original imbalance and deprivation. In the US, where civil rights changes have led to vastly increased representation of black people in areas formerly closed to them, this has not significantly changed conditions for the masses.

Further, there are those who argue that deprivation suffered by any person in society has to be dealt with, regardless of ethnic connection. Is the unemployed white youngster, for example, any less discriminated against than the unemployed black youngster? Severe deprivation in any section of society must be tackled, they believe, and not just the deprivation that results from racial discrimination.

> **'Positive discrimination is an attempt to counter disadvantage by equalizing provision.'**
> Issues and Resources, *AFFOR*

discrimination?

'It's just another kind of racism.'
Unemployed school-leaver

Multi-cultural

At one time it was generally assumed that the correct education for children from ethnic minorities was to integrate them as speedily as possible into the 'host' culture – which often meant the disappearance of the minority culture. Teaching was determinedly ethnocentric – that is, designed from the viewpoint of the dominant culture.

However, in recent years, people have started to discuss instead what form of education is best suited to eradicating prejudice and discrimination in the long term. In any anti-racist strategy, education of the new generations looms large.

Multi-culturalism One solution is to design curricula which are consciously multi-cultural, and do not start from an ethnocentric viewpoint. They would include teaching about other cultures, religions and societies.

Many agree that this is a component of the right kind of education, but that it is not its only aspect. Taken on its own, they argue, it can be another form of tokenism. It may do no more than present a 'let's all get to know each other' approach, without developing in pupils an ability for independent, critical thought about

> 'We may preach equality, but if we practise discrimination, the hypocritical lesson will not fail to be learned.' Dr Ashley Montagu, anthropologist

education?

the information they receive, or enabling them to cope with prejudice when they encounter it in the world outside school.

Others believe that multi-culturalism should be complemented by measures to raise pupils' (and teachers') awareness of racism, and of the needs and demands of minorities in society.

Another idea is to employ more teachers from ethnic minorities so as to provide positive images of authority with which children from ethnic minorities can identify, and which all children will learn to respect.

Ethnic demands Throughout the world there is now a more prominent demand by ethnic minorities to assert their cultural heritage and emphasize to their youth a sense of pride in and a knowledge of their own culture.

One aspect of this is the attempt to include mother-tongue teaching in schools – that is, to teach not only the dominant language of the country, but also the mother tongue of ethnic minorities; and further, not only to teach the language but also to teach some subjects in the language. Many believe there would be a positive advantage in using the skills that children possess to enrich and increase the awareness, knowledge and communication of all children within a school, not merely those from the ethnic minority. Yet problems arise about how to do this without detriment to the teaching of the dominant language, or to other important learning experiences.

Opposite Displays of different Asian languages are part of special teaching aids in a typical Bradford school with a high proportion of Asian children.

Left An aspect of multi-cultural education – a Nigerian storyteller with London schoolchildren.

Minority politics

Fighting racism, some say, is not just about education and laws. It is also being able to sustain both protest against inequalities and demands for improved conditions. One option is to work through existing political structures, such as political parties or workers' organizations.

What, however, if prejudice and discrimination effectively close off access to these forms of activity for ethnic minorities? The only option may be organization of the ethnic group by itself, for itself. And there are other grounds, as well, on which some argue that there should be separate organizations for ethnic minorities – separate pressure groups, trade unions or political parties.

Creating the right conditions? For a variety of reasons, ethnic minorities are often unwilling to involve themselves in political or protest activity of a more general kind. This may be the result of alienation from the dominant culture, and therefore from its organizations. It may be because of linguistic and cultural barriers. It may be because they do not believe that change will ever come. Having separate organizations, it is argued, will create conditions under which people who feel like this may be encouraged to become more involved, and lend their pressure to the work of bringing change.

Some believe that this form of separate organization is the objective in itself; others, that it is only a means to an end. The next step would be an alliance, and ultimately a fusion, of these minority organizations with those of the rest of society.

Black Power? One style of ethnic power movement developed during the massive civil rights campaign in the US in the 1950s and 1960s. Numbers of white civil rights workers were also involved in all aspects of the campaign.

Towards the end of the campaign, however, some black people began to question the wisdom of this, and the 'Black Power' movement emerged. In *Black Protest* Joanne Grant describes how: 'It took away the right of white staff members to vote at staff meetings, thereby in effect driving them from the organization. The theory was that Negroes must organize Negroes to help bring about an increase in respect for blackness, and that whites must organize in the white community to build a base for the future formation of a coalition of poor whites and poor blacks.'

The Black Power programme included political and economic power, improved self-image, militant black leadership, and mobilizing black consumer power.

Increasing divisions? Critics of separate organization stress that separation will only exacerbate divisions and fuel misunderstandings. The problems of ethnic minorities, they say, are just one aspect of the problems faced by the working class in society. A unified class front across all race divisions is needed. They argue that any departure from this splits the only force capable of achieving change, and thus renders the likelihood of change more remote.

Should people from minority ethnic groups take part in mainstream political and trade union organizations, as here? Or should they organize themselves separately?

'We have to wage a battle on the right for black people to organize themselves as they see fit.'

Stokely Carmichael, US Black Power spokesman

'We don't want segregation and apartheid or second-class members.'

Speaker at British Labour Party conference, on a separate section for blacks

A race war?

In a book called *The Race War*, written in the mid 1960s, Ronald Segal predicted that conflict throughout the world, already drawn along lines of colour, would explode into race war. The non-whites, he argued, are the poor of the world, and the gap between the industrialized nations and the underdeveloped nations was becoming greater. Thus, he predicted, racial tensions were the greatest threat to world peace.

> 'The struggle between whites and non-whites is the major preoccupation of mankind.'
>
> Ronald Segal in The Race War

At the time he was writing, the American South was seeing the culmination of the movement for civil rights for black people; there was the war in Vietnam; and there had been eruptions of violent conflict in various parts of Africa as countries struggled to achieve independence from colonial domination. He saw all these conflicts as characterized essentially by racial divisions. He described the war in Vietnam, for example, by saying that 'white Americans' are fighting 'coloured Asians in the field and bombing them from the air'.

Economic motives? Although his analysis has many supporters, many others believe it was incorrect at the time, and has not been justified by subsequent events. The lines of conflict may be drawn along racial divisions, but the source of such conflict, they argue, is not race hostility. It stems from more fundamental questions about the control of political power and economic resources.

The Americans, for example, did not fight in Vietnam because they wanted to fight Asians. They fought because, in their opinion, the Vietnamese people and their political and economic system, socialism, were a fundamental threat to American capitalism at home and abroad. Whites fight blacks in Kenya, the Congo and Mozambique, not because one side is white and the other is black, but because of economic motives, the wish to control land, resources and people.

In the opinion of Steve Biko, a black political leader who died while in detention for opposing apartheid in South Africa: 'There is no doubt that the colour question in South African politics was originally introduced for economic reasons.'

Underlying causes? Those who oppose the idea that conflict in the world is predominantly a question of race are not, in the main, denying that racial prejudice is a real problem, or that it should be taken seriously. They argue that it is more a question of recognizing its underlying causes, and these they see in economic and political structures, and in the conflicting interests of those who benefit or are disadvantaged by different economic systems and resulting power structures.

Would conflict have been any less where countries are throwing off colonial rule had the colonizer and the colonized been of the same colour? Do you think the search for colonies would have ended any differently had the peoples of Africa been white rather than black?

> 'Economic interest is the most fundamental cause of conflict in the world.'
>
> G.A. Cowan, economist

Reference

Racial classification

In the seventeenth century it was generally believed that humankind was made up of a single species. Such analysis as there was was based on the premise that all humans were of the same species, although their appearance was altered by different climates.

The end of the eighteenth century saw the first attempts to define the position of the people in other parts of the world in relation to the peoples of Europe. This paralleled the growing economic relations between Europe and the rest of the world (see pp 56-59).

Permanent human types By the first half of the nineteenth century, interest in human variety had grown substantially and generated many theories about the diversity of peoples.

A typical stylized classification of different races.

By the middle years of the century, a clear theory of 'permanent human types' had emerged. The idea seems to have originated with a French anatomist called Cuvier, who believed that humankind could be divided into three distinct types in hierarchical order, with 'whites' at the top and 'blacks' at the bottom. The idea quickly spread through Europe and to the United States. It was most systematically expounded in a book by Nott and Gliddon published in Philadelphia in 1884, called *Types of Mankind*.

The theory was that humankind is made up of a finite number of types or 'races' which have permanent differences, and that these differences affect relationships between members of the different races.

As exploration and colonial enterprise resulted

in more and more information on the variety of the world's peoples, it became fashionable to construct typologies of the range of humankind. Tables of the types or races of people were arranged according to their attributes. There was much measuring and comparison of skull and brain size and other physical characteristics.

Darwin's challenge Darwin's ideas on evolution challenged the idea that there was any such thing as a 'permanent type' in nature, and showed that species were not permanent entities, but were continually evolving by adaptation and selection.

Yet the idea of permanent human types continued, and was widely applied. Physical characteristics were linked with mental and behavioural characteristics and used to justify not only the ranking of human beings as inherently superior or inferior, but also the economic relations between them – for example between slave-owners and slaves, colonizer and colonized.

Anthropologists generally worked with this concept and tried merely to establish firmer criteria for defining different races.

Genetics From the 1930s onwards, the development of biological sciences, particularly genetics, led to a fuller investigation of the differences between groups of human beings. The conclusion was that the concept of race cannot be scientifically substantiated.

Biologically, a race is simply a 'breeding population in which there is a greater frequency of distinctive inherited traits than in other breeding populations'. But definitions of races will vary according to which distinctive inherited traits are being analyzed. For example, scientists looking at how a population has adapted to sunlight will emerge with categories in which skin colour is significant. But if they are looking at differences in blood type, they will come up with a different set of categories.

Nevertheless, the type of classification which implies clearly definable racial types is still frequently found in anthropology texts – particularly in summaries of the subject for schools. A great many people take it for granted that the concept of 'race' corresponds to some clearly definable and measurable reality.

MAMMALIA.

ORDER 1. PRIMATES

Fore-teeth cutting; upper 4, parallel; teats & pectoral.

1. HOMO.

Sapiens. Diurnal; varying by education and situation
2. Four-footed, mute, hairy — *Wild Man.*
3. Copper-coloured, choleric, erect. — *American.*
    Hair black, straight, thick; *nostrils* wide, *face* harsh; *beard* scanty; *obstinate*, content free. *Paints* himself with fine red lines. *Regulated* by customs.
4. Fair, sanguine, brawny. — *European.*
    Hair yellow brown, flowing; *eyes* blue; *gentle*, acute, inventive. *Covered* with close vestments. *Governed* by laws.
5. Sooty, melancholic, rigid — *Asiatic.*
    Hair black; *eyes* dark; *severe*, haughty, covetous. *Covered* with loose garments. *Governed* by opinions.
6. Black, phlegmatic, relaxed. — *African.*
    Hair black, frizzled; *skin* silky; *nose* flat; *lips* tumid; *crafty*, indolent, negligent. *Anoints* himself with grease. *Governed* by caprice.

FROM LINNAEUS' *SYSTEMA NATURAE*, 1735

The Swedish botanist Linnaeus (1707-78) produced this classification of humans as well as his more famous plant classifications. Such attempts to categorize along 'scientific' lines were common in the eighteenth and nineteenth centuries.

Europe as colonizer

A reason for racism? One of the reasons most frequently given for modern racism is that it is a legacy from the period of colonialism and slavery, when Europeans explored and settled in large numbers in countries outside Europe. They dominated the world economically and politically, and subjugated numerous people to their rule.

In the opinion of many experts, racism arose as a justification for this, and the ways in which it is expressed in the modern world have a direct link with the attitudes generated in that period.

On the following pages there is a brief résumé of how European colonialism developed and led to the slave trade in African peoples destined for the colonial plantations.

This map of Africa in 1914 shows how almost the entire continent was under the control of European powers.

Africa in 1914

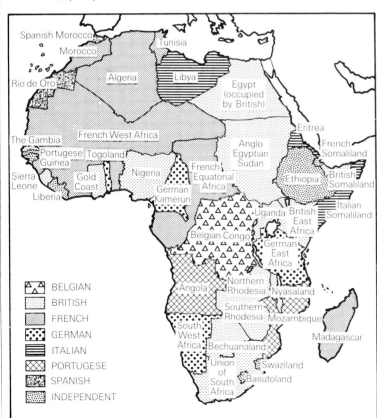

BELGIAN
BRITISH
FRENCH
GERMAN
ITALIAN
PORTUGESE
SPANISH
INDEPENDENT

The Americas

15th century 1492: Columbus, in search of gold and the riches of India, begins his first journey to the Americas. As soon as he returns to Spain (1494), the Pope decrees that the newly discovered territories should be divided into two: the eastern part to belong to Portugal, the western part to Spain. All inhabitants of these new lands were to be converted to the Catholic faith.

16th century Colonization of the large West Indian islands begins with settlers from Spain in search of gold and other precious metals. The empire expands as the Aztec civilization in Mexico and the Inca civilization in Peru are conquered.
1530 onwards: Spaniards face increasing rivalry from other Europeans – the French, English and Dutch, looking for profitable trading opportunities.

17th century A second stream of settlers begins to populate the Americas, mainly English and French, in search of precious metals, then trade, fishing and farming. They settle mainly on the smaller islands of the Antilles and along the eastern seaboard of North America, seizing land from the Amerindians. By the papal decree of 1494, Portugal holds Brazil, concentrating on sugar production there.

Africa

15th century The Portuguese begin exploring the coast, looking for trade, minerals and religious converts. 1441: They bring the first African slaves to Europe from West Africa.
1498: Vasco da Gama rounds the southern tip of Africa and opens up the east coast, and profitable Indian Ocean trade between Africa and Asia, to the Portuguese, who seize their first territories on the East African coast.

16th century The transatlantic slave trade begins from West Africa to the new American colonies.
1571: The Portuguese start to conquer Angola.

17th century The Dutch, French, Danes, English and Portuguese compete for trade along the West African coast.

1652: The first Dutch settlers land in South Africa.

18th century The transatlantic slave trade and other profitable trading increases. Many European nations are involved.

19th century 1806: The British annex the Dutch colony at the Cape of Good Hope in South Africa.
1830s: The French capture Algiers and begin to conquer Algeria.
Exploration of the interior of Africa increases, together with considerable Christian missionary activity. Towards the end of the century Britain and France annex territory in West Africa. Mainly from 1884 onwards, there is a scramble to seize territories in Africa by other European powers. By 1914 the continent has been divided between a few colonial powers (see map).

India
This part of the world had been explored by Europeans for trade since the discovery of the sea route round Africa. The opening up of both America and Africa to Europe had been prompted by the search for routes to the east.

17th century The British East India Company is formed to seize the profitable Indian trade from the Portuguese.

18th century To secure its wealth, the Company seizes territories in India. By the nineteenth century Britain rules almost the entire subcontinent.

Australia and New Zealand
Australia is settled from the end of the eighteenth century to the middle of the nineteenth century by British settlers, and New Zealand from the first quarter of the nineteenth century.
Both the Aborigines in Australia and the Maoris in New Zealand are subjugated, and driven from their land.

Former colonies often still carry an economic legacy from the days of colonialism. They may be dependent on the production and export of just one product – a pattern established to suit the needs of the colonial power.

Proportion of income derived from one product

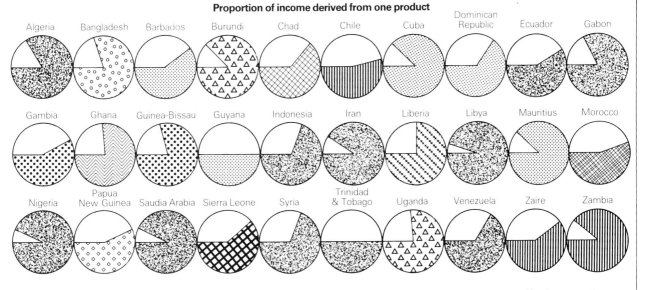

KEY: each circle represents the total export income of that country and the shaded portion represents the share of this earned by the one product

 sugar and honey   oil seed and nuts   cotton   petroleum

precious stones   non-ferrous ores   copper/copper ore   iron ore/concentrates

 cocoa   crude fertilisers   coffee   jute and jute products

The transatlantic slave trade

15th century The Portuguese take slaves – bought or captured in West Africa – to work on Portuguese sugar plantations in the Azores and Madeira.
With the growth of Spanish settlements in the West Indies and Central and South America, labour is needed for the gold and silver mines and sugar plantations. The slave trade increases.

17th century By the middle of the century, the Dutch, English and French have all seized territory in America. European demand rises for the sugar, tea, coffee, cotton and tobacco produced in the colonies. The demand for slave labour rises with it.

18th century Most European countries are now taking part in the slave trade, partnered by West African kings and merchants. Great wealth is made from it.
In the so-called 'triangular trade', the ships make three journeys: from Europe, carrying manufac-tured goods to West Africa, to exchange these goods for slaves; from West Africa to America, to sell the slaves; and from America back to Europe, laden with plantation products – sugar, rum, cotton, tobacco – produced by the slaves.

Anti-slavery movement and abolition From the start, slaves rebel against their condition. They resist capture in Africa, fight on slave ships, escape from the plantations. Communities of escaped slaves survive for some time in central Jamaica, Surinam and Brazil. There are many slave risings as well, although few are successful. Most are put down with utmost brutality. But in San Domingo, led by the former slave Toussaint L'Ouverture,

A typical advertisement. Slave auctions were common throughout the southern states of America in the first half of the nineteenth century.

SLAVES AT SALE
WITHOUT RESERVE.

BY BEARD, CALHOUN & CO.
J. A. BEARD, Auctioneer.

WILL BE SOLD AT AUCTION ON
TUESDAY, Jan. 16th,

AT 12 O'CLOCK, AT BANKS' ARCADE, THE FOLLOWING DESCRIBED NEGROES:

1. ROSIN, 13 years of age, a griffe, good house boy, fine temper, fully guarantied, and speaks German and English.

2. JORDAN, 23 years of age, a likely negro house servant and trusty waiter, fully guarantied.

3. JANE, aged 24 years, a very superior washer, ironer, good American cook, and House Woman, fully guarantied.

4. MARY, aged 24 years, and child 1 year old, a trusty woman, good washer, ironer and American cook fully guarantied.

5. EDWIN, aged 27 years, a griffe man, an excellent waiter, steward and trusty servant fully guarantied.

6. ESTHER, aged 40 years, a smart intelligent and cleanly cook, washer and ironer, title only guarantied.

7. ANNE, aged 24 years, an excellent house servant, washer, ironer, and good cook, with her three children, one aged 5 another 2 and the last 1 year; they are fully guarantied but will be sold to go into the country, by her owner's instructions.

8. SAM, aged 28 years, a field hand; title only guarantied.

9. AGNES, aged 24 years, a good cook, washer and ironer, fully guarantied.

10. HENRY, aged about 26 years, a field hand, and a stout man, sold as having run away from the plantation.

11. JOHN, aged 15 years, a smart waiting boy, fully guarantied.

12. JANE, aged 17 years, a fine house girl and field hand fully guarantied.

13. MARY, aged 35 years, superior nurse and house woman, fully guarantied.

ALSO:

14. PATRICK, aged 28 years a likely man good barber, body and house servant. Sold under a good character, and fully guarantied against the vices and maladies prescribed by law.

TERMS CASH. Acts of sale before J. R. BEARD, Notary Public at the expense of the purchasers.

ALSO,

The following described Slaves sold for account of Mr. Henry Deacon, who failed to comply with the terms of sale made for the account of the Succession of C. H. L. ELWYN, deceased, to wit:
The Negress MATHILDA, aged about 29 years and her son PAUL, 7 years-a good washer, Ironer and Cooker.

TERMS CASH. Acts of sale before H. B. CENAS, Notary Public, at the expense of the purchasers.

slaves establish the independent repubic of Haiti.

Towards the end of the eighteenth century a number of pressures to end the slave trade come together. The economic interests of Britain, one of the main slaving nations, are changing. She is becoming more an industrial nation and less a farming one. Her trading interests are also changing – the trade with North America is less important, and that with India and East Asia more so. Manufacturers and traders begin to think that slavery is an inefficient way of producing goods, compared with using labourers who work voluntarily for a wage and can move freely as their labour is needed.

At the same time, humanitarian and moral objections are growing; people campaign against the immorality of putting another human being into slavery.

During the early years of the nineteenth century, these pressures prompt some nations to make the trade illegal – although it continues illegally into the 1860s. The struggle for emancipation takes longer. From the 1830s onwards, first Britain, then France and most South American countries declare all slaves free. Cuba, the United States and Brazil do not, and it is only in the 1880s that the slave system finally comes to an end.

Over a period of 350 years it is estimated that nearly ten million people were taken from Africa and shipped as slaves across the Atlantic.

African and European traders haggle about prices and inspect the slaves at the market in Zanzibar, off the East African coast, 1840s.

Glossary

Anthropologist – Someone who studies the science of humankind

Anti-semitism – Prejudice and hostility towards Jews

Apartheid – South Africa's official policy of racial segregation. *See also* Segregation

Assimilation – Absorption of a group – its culture, way of life, even (through sexual mixing over many generations) of its colour

Citizen – An official member of a country or state

Civil rights – Rights as a citizen of a country

Classification – Arranging things or people in classes, each class being defined as having items with the same or similar characteristics

Colony – A settlement in a country which is wholly or partly controlled and ruled by another country

Discrimination – Treating someone differently from others

Ethnic group – A group of people defined by religious and cultural characteristics, as well as those believed to be racial, eg. skin colour

Franchise – The right to vote

Gene – An element in a germ cell, transmitted by the parent, which gives a person hereditary characteristics

Genetics – The study of heredity and variation in life forms

Immigrant – Someone who enters a country of which he or she is not a native, in order to work and live there

Integration – Mixing and cooperation between different groups in work, housing, leisure etc.

Migrant – Someone who moves from one place to another to settle

Missionary – A person who goes to another country to teach a religion and try to make converts to it

Prejudice – Preconceived, biased beliefs, not based on actual knowledge

Race relations – Relations between people who are said to be of different races

Racism – Negative attitudes and/or behaviour towards people believed to be of another race

Scapegoat – Someone who bears the blame for things they are not responsible for

Segregation – Physical separation of groups from each other in one or all spheres of life

Stereotype – A standardized, fixed image or conception of people which is applied to all people in that category

Useful addresses

AFFOR (All Faiths For One Race) 173 Lozells Road, Lozells, Birmingham B19 1RN. Provides information and materials on race relations and racism in Britain, and on Asian and Afro-Caribbean communities. Produces its own publications.

ALTARF (All London Teachers Against Racism and Fascism) Lambeth Teachers' Centre, Santley Street, London SW4. Produces materials on race and racism in schools.

Commission for Racial Equality (CRE) Elliott House, 10/12 Allington Street, London SW1E 5EH. An organization set up by the Race Relations Act, 1976, to eliminate racial discrimination, promote equality of opportunity, and operate the legislation on race relations. It provides its own publications, and has a library on many race relations issues and questions of interest in multiracial Britain, including education. CRE also provides information, including a wide variety of free guidance leaflets on the terms and application of the Race Relations Act of 1976. Can supply a full list of local Community Relations Councils throughout Britain.

Commonwealth Institute Kensington High Street, London W8. Supplies information on Commonwealth countries and their cultures, including a wide range of materials available on loan. Also covers education in multiracial schools.

Institute of Race Relations 247 Pentonville Road, London N1 9NG. Provides books and own publications on race relations in Britain and internationally. These include pamphlets for schools.

Minority Rights Group Benjamin Franklin House, 36 Craven Street, London WC2 5NG. An international human rights group and educational charity which monitors conditions for minority groups all over the world. Publications, including its own reports, are available.

Runnymede Trust Information Office, 37A Grays Inn Road, London WC1. Provides information on race relations in Britain and the EEC.

Further reading

Edward Brathwaite and Anthony Phillips, *The People Who Came Book 3* (Longman Caribbean, 1972). A useful and succinct illustrated history of the Americas over the last 200 years. It covers the period when the new countries established by European settlers began to try and free themselves from the political and cultural influence of Europe, and when the abolition of slavery and emancipation of slaves was achieved.

Dee Brown, *Wounded Knee* (Fontana Lions, 1979). A history of the American West from the Amerindian point of view, drawn from first-hand accounts of the great Indian leaders. It documents the Indians' struggle against the settlers from 1860 to 1890.

Nigel File and Chris Power, *Black Settlers in Britain 1555-1958* (Heinemann Educational Books, 1981). A fascinating documentation of the life and conditions of black settlers in Britain over 400 years, using contemporary facsimile documents and illustrations.

Patterns of Racism and *Roots of Racism* (Institute of Race Relations, 1982). Two books illustrated with contemporary material which explore racism today as a legacy of the economic and political relationships between Europe and the rest of the world during the past 400 years.

Children under Apartheid (International Defence and Aid Fund, 1980). Photographic and textual documentation of children in South Africa and how they are both reacting to their conditions and organizing against them.

Julius Lester, *To Be a Slave* (Puffin, 1968). An anthology on the history of slavery.

Patricia Patterson and James Carnegie, *The People Who Came, Book 2* (Longman Caribbean, 1970). An illustrated history of the first encounters between European settlers and the Amerindians in the Americas, the subsequent settlement of the continent and the beginnings of the slave trade.

Films

(See right for film distributors)

Blacks Britannica (1978; available from Other Cinema in 16mm). A documentary about racism in Britain from the point of view of black working-class people.

Divide and Rule – Never! (Newsreel Collective; available from Other Cinema in 16mm, Concord in 16mm and video). A film which explores the issues of race and young people in relation to school, employment and the law. It was made by young people for young people. Support materials by Newsreel Collective are available from ALTARF (see p.61).

Generations of Resistance (available from Other Cinema in 16mm). Uses rare newsreel film to trace the history of the African peoples' struggle against colonialism and the South African régime from 1906 to 1976.

Immigration (Mary Glasgow Publications: in filmstrip and cassette tape). A useful visual introduction to the subject of immigration to the UK. Available from AFFOR (see p.61).

It Ain't Half Racist, Mum (Campaign Against Racism in the Media/BBC Open Door, 1979; available from Concord and Other Cinema in 16mm and video). Explores both the subtly implicit and the overt racism of everyday television programmes, ranging from comedy to current affairs.

Our People (six films by Thames Television, 1978; available from Film Forum in 16mm). Subjects covered include immigration and immigrants in relation to law, employment and housing in the UK and Europe; the history of the British Empire and its impact on multiracial Britain; and the effects of racism and the work to combat it.

Step Forward Youth (Black Arts, 1977; available from Other Cinema in 16mm). A documentary about racism as experienced by black youth in London.

Why prejudice? (BBC Schools, 1980; available from Concord in 16mm and video). Students, including a Scottish boy who came south, describe racial prejudice they have experienced and explore why people feel prejudice.

Film distributors

Concord Films Council 201 Felixstowe Road, Ipswich, Suffolk IP3 9BJ

Film Forum (DBW) 56 Brewer Street, London W1R 3FA

The Other Cinema 79 Wardour Street, London W1V 3TH

Index

Credits

The author and publishers would
like to thank the following for
their kind permission to
reproduce copyright illustrations:

Aldus Archive: 12, 30
Associated Press: 27
Barnaby's Picture Library: 7
Nick Birch: 37
Camera Press: 6, 24-5, 28-9, 38-9,
    40, 41, 42-3, 44-5, 48
Mary Evans Picture Library: 14,
    15, 16, 17, 59
Francis Fashesin: 47
S & R. Greenhill: 5, 8-9, 49
Barbara Heller Photo Library: 20
    ©Robert Aberman
Mansell Collection: 58
Peter Newark's Western
    Americana: 13
Photosource: 32
Pitt Rivers Museum, C. Smith
    Collection: 18
Popperfoto: 31, 34
Mark Rusher (I.F.L.): 51
Tony Stone Picture Library: cover
Topham Picture Library: 26
Alexander Turnbull Library, N.Z.:
    19
United Nations Photo: 33
Mike Wells 'Save the Children': 53
Wiener Library: 11, 22
    ©Bundesarchiv Koblenz, 23

The illustrations on pages 54, 56
and 57 were drawn by the
Maltings Partnership.

Picture research by Diana Morris.
Design by Norman Reynolds.